Preface

Eighty per cent of the land area of Britain is rural by use ... ce and almost a fifth of the British population lives in rural se ... Yet, very little published material exists about the planning of such areas, compared to the volume of literature on urban planning. This publication attempts to reduce the imbalance a little by reviewing, from a geographical angle, the methods and approaches used for the drawing up of policies in county development plans and for the preparation of village plans. It can only go part way towards an understanding of the planning issues facing villages and rural communities at the present time. It does not attempt to cover all policies and plans of every rural county in Britain, although material was initially collected from all but a handful of counties. Obviously not every county could be used for illustration, and to those counties with little or scant mention, I apologise. As few structure plans have as yet been formally approved, I have used little information from this source; it is, moreover, perhaps too early to appreciate fully whether fresh approaches towards the planning of rural settlements are consistently and comprehensively being carried out, especially at district level.

I would like to acknowledge the encouragement and advice given by Professor John House during the various stages in the preparation of this publication; his careful editing has been much appreciated. I must also thank my head of department, Professor J. H. Bird, for financial assistance towards the travel costs, and also members of the Cartographic Unit, University of Southampton, for the drawing of the maps. Thanks are also extended to the Librarian and staff at the Department of the Environment for providing me with access to county development plans, to various officers in the DOE for helpful discussions and, not least, to the county planning officers and assistants who have searched out information and documents and answered many questions.

B.J.W.

Contents

1 Introduction

Rural settlements have long been a source of interest and a field of research for geographers. In Britain, research has been largely historically biased, whereas studies of contemporary rural settlements, their recent development and their integration into broader socio-economic systems, are scarce by comparison. There is considerable scope here for geographical research, as has been illustrated by recent publications (Best and Rogers 1973, Jones 1973, and Moseley 1974). In contrast, the volume of travel literature on villages continues to grow—evidence of an increasing public interest in the countryside and in the architectural heritage to be found in British villages (Hale 1971-75).

This book is essentially a review of planning policies and village plans over the period since the Town and Country Planning Act of 1947. It relies for its source material not on published geographical literature but on County Development Plans and on planning reports or studies. The aim is to identify the various types of policy and plan adopted and used by local planning authorities, and to discuss these in relation to the patterns of population change during this period. In order to do this, it is expedient to describe some of the methods of survey and analysis used, to consider some of the essential problems for which policies have been devised, to discuss the difficulties in interpretation and implementation of policies, and to outline some possible directions for future policies. The effectiveness of such policies and plans is outside the scope of this book, which concentrates on the spatial characteristics of policies and on the geographical features of plans, appreciating at the same time that there are other viewpoints which are equally valid.

Theory relevant to rural settlement planning

In general there has been little reference to settlement theory in the preparation of policies and plans for villages and rural areas, though it could be argued that there is little relevant theory available. Certainly there is a distinct lack of theory compared to what is available for urban areas and cities. Nevertheless, there exists some theory which, if not entirely derived from investigations of rural settlements, is of significance in understanding the structure and the functions of rural settlements, and is therefore of importance in their planning. In addition, there exist a number of basic principles, used by planning authorities but not built into any coherent theory, which have been effective in directing the recent development of villages and small towns.

The theory associated with the location and status of central places would seem to be an essential starting point for planning the size, functions and growth patterns of settlement in any rural sub-region or in the rural parts of city-regions. Furthermore, an understanding of the relative degree of centrality of any given village or country town might be seen as crucial for the determination of its future role in the region, for its development as a central place or as a location for population growth. Curiously enough, there has been little resort to central place theory as conceived by Christaller (1933) but this is not to say that the principles— the hierarchies of central places, the distribution and location of particular grades of central place and the complementary tributary areas—have not been recognized in policies and plans. Indeed they have, but the fundamental classifications of settlements have been much closer to the central place work of Dickinson and Bracey rather than that of Christaller. Dickinson (1947) based his grades of settlements on the types of function present and on their spheres of influence, criteria which have been adopted by many rural planning authorities in order to classify settlements. Bracey's work (1953, 1956) in south-west England followed similar lines.

The key settlement concept uses some principles of central place theory and assumes that the focussing of services, facilities and employment in one selected settlement will satisfy the essential needs of the surrounding villages and hamlets and that in the long term such concentration is more economic than the dispersion of facilities. It has been widely used throughout Britain in areas which differ considerably from one another in respect of population trends. Key settlements tend not to have a particular slot in the hierarchy of central places, nor have their service areas or spheres of influence been carefully defined or measured.

Another aspect of theoretical work centres on the threshold concept. The basic tenet of this concept is that as settlements expand, growth is subject to a series of economic limitations, each of which must be surmounted before growth can occur. These limitations are usually expressed in financial terms, such as the cost of a village by-pass. This concept has the advantage that it allows alternative developments to be compared economically, but one disadvantage is that it is difficult to write in social or aesthetic controls (Aberdeen 1972). Moreover, thresholds can change over time, as standards are raised or modified.

The forerunner of the threshold concept has been the constraint-capacity theme, which has conditioned policy statements for many rural settlements. The essence of this approach is that settlements are defined in terms of their suitability for change or growth using a part-subjective, part-objective assessment of the factors influencing development. In one case the influence may be relatively easily measured—such as the physical capacity of a sewerage system; in another situation the constraints may be qualitative—such as grade of agricultural land, or townscape character. Further problems with this approach are that the capacities of different controls—schools and health services for example—do not always coincide, so that the operation of one system at capacity level may defer efficient use of another. Likewise, physical constraints, such as steep slopes, may prevent full use of existing infrastructure by restricting additional development.

The recognition of areas or morphological units which have some elements in common (e.g. building materials, architectural style, or phase of development) and the identification of the morphological structure of settlements is one aspect of urban geographical theory which is being increasingly used in rural planning, especially in the establishment of conservation and policy areas.

Finally, a number of principles originate in government circulars and policy notes and act as guidelines for planning rural areas. It suffices to mention two: in meeting the need for development, good agricultural land should not be wasted and the countryside should not be spoilt; new housing should be located in settlements where supporting services can be provided efficiently. Planning authorities would accept such basic principles almost without question but it is interesting to see how they have been interpreted in policy statements.

Planning of rural settlements therefore has not had a sound theoretical background and the development of theory in geography has not greatly aided the planning process. Nevertheless, the past quarter-century has made its own unmistakeable contribution to Britain's rural heritage, a contribution visually unacceptable to many people but absorbing and stimulating for the applied geographer.

References

Aberdeen C.C. (1972). *Burgh of Ellon—Thresholds of Expansion.*
Best, R. H. and Rogers, A. W. (1973). *The Urban Countryside,* Faber and Faber.
Bracey, H. E. (1953). 'Towns as rural service centres—an index of centrality with special reference to Somerset', *Trans. Inst. Brit. Geog.* **19**, 95–105.
– (1956). A rural component of centrality applied to six southern counties in the United Kingdom', *Economic Geography*, **32**, 38–50.
Christaller, W. (1933, 1966). *Central Places in Southern Germany* (English translation), Prentice-Hall.
Dickinson, R. E. (1947). *City, Region and Regionalism,* Routledge and Kegan Paul.
Hale, Robert, publishers (1971–75). The Village Series—*Villages in Devon,* by S. H. Burton, and other volumes.
Jones, G. (1973). *Rural Life,* Longman.
Moseley, M. J. (1974). *Growth Centres in Spatial Planning,* Pergamon.

2 Changes in the distribution of population

The aims and the implementation of planning policies for rural settlements since the 1947 Act cannot be fully appreciated without reference to the changes that have occurred in population distribution. Three broad trends of change or redistribution may be recognized.

Firstly, many changes have come about as a result of pressures external to rural areas. Urban areas faced with housing problems or with growth in employment have looked to neighbouring rural areas for residential land and many rural settlements have experienced pressures for private development to accommodate a commuting population. Consequently, planning authorities have had to determine settlements appropriate for growth, decide on the scale of growth and adopt policies to integrate the new development. Complementary to such growth policies have been restraint policies for unsuitable settlements and landscape conservation policies.

Secondly, there are those changes related to internal adjustments in the rural economy—such as the decrease in primary employment—which have given rise to out-migration and depopulation. Policies for such areas have varied from the adoption of potential growth points to a realistic rationalization of the settlement pattern. And finally there are those changes resulting from the implementation of special policies: these include policies for the establishment of new villages and policies relating to the re-location or abandonment of settlements.

In contrast to these policies for changes in population distribution, most planning authorities have operated policies to maintain stable situations in certain villages and hamlets. The reasons for such policies have often been local ones—school size or lack of public utilities; although zonal controls—beautiful landscape or green belts—have also been widely applied.

An appreciation of the changes in population that have occurred in rural districts and in the smaller country towns since 1947 may be gained from an analysis of trends over the inter-censal periods of 1951--61 and 1961--71.

During these two decades the character of many small country towns and villages has altered substantially, to the extent that some settlements are now hardly rural in any respect. Other rural settlements have shown little change and are still rural in the traditional sense. But taking England, Wales and Scotland together, the population in rural districts

TABLE 1

Population in Rural and County Districts

in 1000s	1951	1961	Change 1951–61 (%)	1971	Change 1961–71 (%)
England	7428	8176	+ 10·1	9730	+ 19·0
Wales	766	778	+ 1·6	838	+ 7·7
Scotland	1475	1472	− 0·2	1527	+ 3·8
Total	9669	10 426	+ 7·8	12 095	+ 16·0

Source: Census 1951, 1961 and 1971

is now some 2·5 million more than in 1951—an increase of around 25 per cent. Over two-thirds of this increase has occurred since 1961 (Table 1).

This striking re-distribution in rural districts has been accompanied by a similar pattern of growth in the small towns and market centres, which are an essential part of the rural settlement structure. These small towns, about 500 in total and under 10 000 in population in 1951, have increased in total population by about 30 per cent. Consequently, some are no longer small towns with a limited sphere of influence but are urban centres in their own right. Many, particularly in Scotland and Wales, have continued to lose population or have remained static despite the efforts of various planning bodies to stimulate new employment and encourage renewal of their infrastructure. To a considerable extent, the direction of change in these towns in indicative of and complementary to the economic prosperity and social well-being, or otherwise, of the villages in the surrounding rural areas. Like the rural districts, the greatest proportion of their growth--over 70 per cent--took place in the 1960s (Table 2). Whilst national trends are obviously significant, it is important to identify the trends at the levels at which the planning of rural settlements has taken place, that is, at the rural and county district level.

A simple analysis of the basic trends between the two censal periods allows a six-fold classification to be made:

1. Districts which were decreasing in population between 1951 and 1961, and in which the rate of depopulation increased between 1961 and 1971. These may be termed areas of 'accelerated depopulation'.

TABLE 2

Population in Small Towns

in 1000s	1951	1961	Change 1951–61 (%)	1971	Change 1961–71 (%)
England	1493	1664	+ 11·5	2079	+ 24·9
Wales	297	304	+ 2·6	334	+ 9·8
Scotland	533	546	+ 2·4	596	+ 9·2
Total	2323	2514	+ 8·2	3009	+ 19·7

Source: Census 1951, 1961 and 1971

TABLE 3

Trends of population change, 1951-61-71

	Rural & County Districts in			Total	
	England (%)	Wales (%)	Scotland (%)	No.	%
Accelerated depopulation	4·4	22·0	34·3	99	14·9
Reduced depopulation	7·8	22·0	22·2	89	13·3
Reversed depopulation	23·2	23·7	15·7	140	21·0
Reversed growth	2·2	6·8	9·1	31	4·6
Reduced growth	14·9	6·8	7·6	80	12·0
Accelerated growth	47·5	18·7	11·1	228	34·2
	100·0	100·0	100·0	667	100·0

Source: Census 1951, 1961 and 1971

2. Districts which were decreasing in population between 1951 and 1961, and in which the rate of depopulation slackened in the 1961-71 period. These are areas of 'reduced depopulation'.
3. Districts where population was decreasing in the 1951-61 period but in which the trend was reversed in the 1961-71 period. These are areas of 'reversed depopulation'.
4. Districts which were increasing in population between 1951 and 1961 but in which population decreased in the 1961-71 period. These may be termed areas of 'reversed growth'.
5. Districts in which population was increasing between 1951 and

1961 and in which the rate of population increase dropped over the 1961-71 period. Such areas have shown a trend of 'reduced growth'.

6. Districts which have increased in population during both periods but in which the rate of increase rose in the 1961-71 period. These are areas of 'accelerated growth'.

The proportions of rural and county districts in these six classes are shown in Table 3.

Although the national trend is one of growth in rural areas, it is plainly evident from the above table that almost a third of all rural districts are continuing to lose population. Perhaps the most significant trend is that 21 per cent of districts reversed their decline in population and a further 13 per cent reduced the rate of decline. Another noteworthy feature is the number of districts which increased their rate of growth—228—of which most are in England. Figs. 1 and 2 show the distribution of the six categories throughout England and Wales, and Scotland respectively.

Areas of accelerated depopulation are to be found mainly in the upland zones of Scotland and Wales. There are two extensive areas of decline, one of which includes the Grampian Mountains, the Buchan peninsula and Angus. Losses in population in parts of this area exceeded 20 per cent in the 1961-71 period but it is worth noting that several of the small burghs have begun to grow in population or have stemmed their earlier decline. The other extensive tract comprises the core of the Southern Uplands, together with the Cheviot Hills and parts of the northern Pennines. Not all this area is upland, however, since it includes some of the remote coastal lands of south-west Scotland, the Merse in Berwickshire and the lowlands around Carlisle and Penrith. Outside these two main areas there are smaller pockets of accelerating depopulation in central Wales and in scattered rural districts, most of which are relatively remote from urban areas.

Districts which have experienced reduced depopulation tend either to fringe the core areas of depopulation or to be in dispersed and isolated locations where the out-movement of population has slowed down and is stabilizing. The holding action of the planning policies for these areas coupled with increased modern amenities, and especially the growth in personal transport, may well be sufficient for some of these districts to begin to show additions of population in the 1970s.

The number of districts which have reversed-growth trends is small and their locations have little in common.

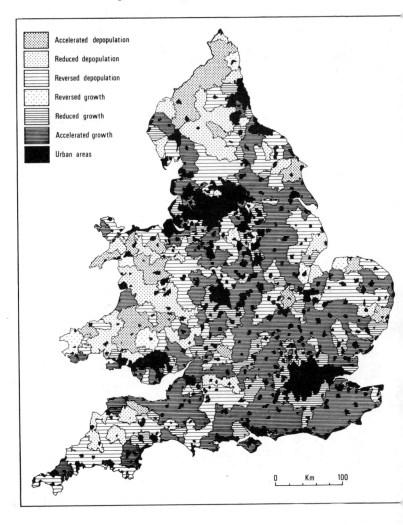

Accelerated depopulation

Reduced depopulation

Reversed depopulation

Reversed growth

Reduced growth

Accelerated growth

Urban areas

0   Km   100

FIG. 1 England and Wales: population trends 1951–61 and 1961–71 (census 1951, 1961 and 1971)

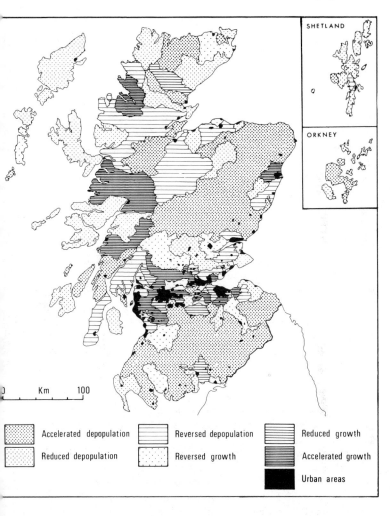

FIG. 2 Scotland: population trends 1951–61 and 1961–71 (census 1951, 1961 and 1971)

TABLE 4

Trends of population change in small towns, 1951–61–71

	Percentage of small towns (under 10 000 pop.)			Total No.	%
	England	*Wales*	*Scotland*		
Accelerated depopulation	3·7	15·9	13·6	42	8·5
Reduced depopulation	2·6	5·8	11·6	29	5·8
Reversed depopulation	16·1	29·0	30·3	111	22·3
Reversed growth	6·2	11·6	10·3	41	8·3
Reduced growth	16·5	11·6	12·3	72	14·5
Accelerated growth	54·9	26·1	21·9	202	40·6
	100·0	100·0	100·0	497	100·0

Source: Census 1951, 1961 and 1971

At the other end of the scale, districts showing growth trends are almost all related to increasing urban influences. The pattern of change suggests that rings of differential growth may be identified around London, the West Midlands conurbation and the West Yorkshire conurbation and to a lesser extent around cities like Nottingham, Bristol, and Gloucester-Cheltenham. The districts which currently have trends of reduced growth tend to lie adjacent to the urban edge, those with accelerating growth are slightly further away and those with reversed depopulation are situated still further out. It is in these outer districts that the role of the small town is important; initially as a centre of employment and services, subsequently encouraging commuting from nearby villages, and ultimately perhaps stimulating employment in the surrounding larger rural settlements.

The next two decades may well see an extention of the trends identified above if the directions of change in the small towns set precedents for change in adjacent rural districts (Table 4).

It is against this background of population change that the policies and plans will be reviewed and discussed.

References

General Register Office, *Census 1951, 1961.*
Office of Population Censuses and Surveys, *Census 1971.*

3 Policies and plans at County and District levels

The apparent division between town and country formed the background to much of the immediate post-war planning theory and legislation. The Scott Committee's recommendations (1942) were realized through the Rural Water Supplies and Sewerage Act (1944), the Education Act (1944), the Agriculture Act (1947), the Town and Country Planning Act (1947), and the National Parks and Access to the Countryside Act (1949). The most significant set of controls was contained in the Town and Country Planning Act, which required local authorities to prepare development plans for their area. Such development plans, prepared at county level and based on a detailed survey, were to indicate the way in which the land in the area should be used. Guidance for the survey and explanations of the way the development plan was to operate followed in a number of Circulars and Advice Notes, the most important of which were Circulars 40 (survey requirements) (M.T.C.P. 1948a) and 59 (location of rural centres) (M.T.C.P. 1948b), and the Advice Note on the Siting of Houses in Country Districts (1950).

Population and service provision

The fundamental theme in all development plans was that of population. As was seen in Chapter 2, there has been an extensive redistribution of population since the War, but very few local authorities anticipated the scale of these changes (Table 5). The difference between the estimated and the actual population is about 18 000 persons—that is 15 per cent above the estimated total. More recently population projections have taken the form of a maximum/minimum approach with the adoption of policies which are flexible enough to accommodate whatever scale of change occurs within these limits. A further amendment, which may well assist accuracy of estimation, is that rural districts and urban areas have been combined to form larger functional areas, for example Worcestershire Structure Plan (1973) forecasts (Table 6).

Whilst this new approach may be an improvement on the former one, it still comprises forecasts for administrative divisions and not for geographical, urban-based or functional sub-regions. Employment structure and its projection have been treated in a similar way to population. It is

TABLE 5

Population change in Worcestershire 1951–71

Rural District	1951 Census	1971 estimates	1971 Census
Bromsgrove	28 172	30 000	36 443
Droitwich	15 464	14 000	14 935
Evesham	16 453	17 000	20 307
Kidderminster	11 299	11 000	12 516
Martley	11 441	12 000	12 861
Pershore	16 355	16 500	20 430
Tenbury	5403	6000	5276
Upton-upon-Severn	15 340	13 500	15 299
	119 927	120 000	138 067

Source: Worcestershire C.C. (1951) and census 1971

TABLE 6

Population forecasts in Worcestershire, 1981 and 1986

Sub Area	1971 Census	1981 low forecast	1981 high forecast	1986 low forecast	1986 high forecast
A	84 896	105 000	110 600	114 700	124 000
B	77 112	93 000	95 000	95 800	98 000
C	40 775	74 500	75 000	81 700	85 000
D	5276	6500	6600	7100	7200
E	57 164	62 000	63 800	64 700	66 000
F		1500	2200	2200	8200
G	82 285	110 000	115 000	116 100	123 400

Sub Area A: Kidderminster M.B. and R.D., Bewdley M.B., and Stourport U.D.
Sub Area B: Bromsgrove U.D. and R.D.
Sub Area C: Redditch U.D.
Sub Area D: Tenbury R.D.
Sub Area E: Martley R.D., Upton-upon-Severn R.D., and Malvern U.D.
Sub Area F: Urban fringe parishes close to Worcester City
Sub Area G: Droitwich M.B. and R.D., Evesham M.B. and R.D., and Pershore R.D.

Source: Worcestershire C.C. 1973

surprising that there should be continued adherence to district administrative divisions, although with reorganization of local government boundaries in 1974 it is hoped that a more realistic approach to rural planning will now be taken.

Having analyzed population data as part of their survey for the first development plans, many authorities then proceeded to an analysis of rural population distribution, and to a consideration of population in relation to facilities and services. Some counties undertook very detailed geographical surveys of villages and hamlets, classifying each settlement in respect of size, location or function. This type of analysis was essential for an understanding of the settlement structure in the county and, subsequently, for a clear set of policies to be drawn up. In Monmouthshire, for example, such a survey emphasized the small size and dispersed nature of settlement in the county (Table 7):

TABLE 7

Monmouthshire—population groupings (size and number of settlements)

Rural District	Over 500	500-401	400-301	300-201	200-101	100-51	Under 50
Abergavenny	1	1	2	0	6	7	8
Monmouth	0	0	0	3	2	8	7
Chepstow	4	1	1	1	6	4	1
Pontypool	1	0	1	1	2	8	2
Magor and St. Mellons	4	1	2	1	7	4	7
Totals	10	3	6	6	23	31	25

Source: Monmouths C.C. 1954

Of considerable relevance to planning proposals and policies were the results of the surveys of services and amenities. The Scott report had emphasized the differences in standards and range of services and amenities between town and country, and had indicated that the country dweller and worker should not be disadvantaged in these respects. For this reason, in many of the reports of survey, planning authorities went to great lengths to accurately record and analyze the number of shops, places of worship, village halls, health facilities, educational facilities, and the presence or lack of utilities such as sewerage, electricity and water supply. For example, Dorset (1952)

TABLE 8

Dorset—piped water supply and sewerage facilities, 1952

Rural District	Piped water supply		Waterborne sewerage	
	Pop. served	% total pop.	Pop. served	% total pop.
Beaminster	2850	35	1800	22
Blandford	4790	55	Nil	0
Bridport	4170	55	1400	18
Dorchester	11 370	70	600	4
Shaftesbury	7740	85	3600	40
Sherborne	4000	65	700	11
Sturminster Newton	8550	95	5800	65
Wareham and Purbeck	11 430	70	2400	15
Wimborne and Cranborne	14 570	70	400	2
Totals	69 470	68	16 700	16

Source: Dorset C.C. 1952

recorded the proportion of population supplied with piped water and served by a waterborne sewerage system (Table 8). With only two-thirds of the population served by piped water supplies and less than one-sixth by waterborne sewerage systems, much of the emphasis in policies for villages in Dorset in the development plan was on the extension of these and other amenities. It was clear that as long as such deficiencies continued, the planning authority could not recommend many villages for further residential development even if there was the demand. This is still the case, with lack of sewerage and other utilities deterring residential development.

Lindsey (1952) carried out a detailed survey of its 429 rural settlements and calculated the average number of persons to each facility or service. Again, arrangement of the information was according to rural district, not functional area, which complicates an interpretation of the results and may account for the wide variation in some of the average values (Table 9).

Such surveys enabled planning authorities to identify settlements and districts with particular service deficiencies, and conversely to recognize areas where services were not being fully utilized, i.e. a factor favouring population growth. Thus it was possible to draw up policies for problem areas, where either development of the necessary facilities or

TABLE 9

Lindsey—average number of persons served by selected services and facilities, 1952

Rural District	Food shops	Agricultural repair depots	Village halls	Resident doctors
Caistor	176	536	1168	4283
Gainsborough	178	700	935	3733
Glanford Brigg	164	1495	1220	5492
Grimsby	206	1103	1518	4050
Horncastle	168	626	2760	1983
Isle of Axholme	129	1148	1532	2004
Louth	203	910	617	5753
Spilsby	188	720	913	3960
Welton	215	1218	812	2910
County	177	872	1047	3580

Source: Lindsey C.C. 1952

rationalization of existing services would be carried out; likewise, potential growth areas and settlements could be determined. In due course this kind of analysis led to a series of settlement classifications, initially based on status of services or functions but later based on potential for residential development. The work of Dickinson (1947) in East Anglia and Bracey (1953, 1956) in south-west England clearly influenced a number of planning authorities in grading service centres. Lindsey recognized five levels of service centre:

1. A Regional centre, 250 000 population and over, with specialized services such as a university, theatres, and central government administration, e.g. Nottingham.
2. A Provincial centre, 60 000 to 100 000 population, with services such as local government administration, further education, a number of cinemas, and serving a radius of 20 to 40 miles, e.g. Lincoln.
3. The District centre of 5000 to 60 000 population, with less specialized services and serving a radius of 10 to 15 miles, e.g. Gainsborough and Louth.
4. The Local centre of 1000 to 5000 population, being the urban village or small market town with a variety of shops, secondary school—often catering for weekly needs in shopping and entertainment over a radius of 5 to 8 miles.

5. The Rural centre of 300 to 1200 population, being a medium or large village self-sufficient in everyday necessities and acting as a service centre for a group of 4 to 6 villages.

These classes were essentially the same as those recognized by Dickinson though it is apparent that these presented Lindsey with several problems, especially at the lower end of the scale where the planning authority had to deal with a large number of small settlements.

Investigation of the relationships between centres and the villages and smaller settlements served by them was not pursued to any depth although certain functional types of settlement were recognized, such as 'self-contained centres' and 'dormitory' villages. The ultimate aim of the policy was to designate some ninety settlements as suitable for further development of services and facilities as well as housing. This selection took into account other factors influencing a settlement's suitability for development, such as physical geographical characteristics and road quality.

This type of policy was very largely a static one: it did not take account of the fact that services and facilities had capacities, that the quality and nature of services were changing, that population was becoming more mobile and that the structure of village populations differed widely and altered with time. Lindsey was not alone in this respect as this kind of policy was adopted in many counties. To the credit of the planning department was the detailed survey carried out, which permitted an identification of seventy-two problems, most of which were analyzed at some length. Those affecting the rural areas included:

1. The economics of providing services to many small and scattered villages.
2. The selection of 'rural service centres'.
3. The smallness and wide spacing of existing 'rural service centres'.
4. The decline in functions of market towns.
5. The lack of sewerage in rural areas.
6. The relationship of education development plan proposals to selected villages.

The policy for Lindsey applied for over twenty years until in 1973 it proved to be in need of revision because of changes in living standards, and in particular population distribution: the 1952 development plan had envisaged an increase of only 15 000 population in the rural districts, whereas by 1971 the increase had been of the order of 40 000.

Two further illustrations relating to the role and status of service centres are worth mentioning. Central place theory revolves around the recognition of different grades of centre and the delineation of the servicing area of a centre, both of which present considerable problems of measurement. In Hertfordshire (1951) the grading of settlements was done by allotting points to particular services and facilities:

Group A   These facilities.are considered to be the ones which are most likely to draw residents to a village: secondary school, bus service every two hours or less, village hall— three points each.

Group B   These facilities which in conjunction with those above enable a village to play a greater part in the rural community than is played by a normal village: daily bus service, doctor's surgery, district nurse, industry employing over five people, sewerage system, playing-field—two points each.

Group C   Facilities which are fairly generally available throughout agricultural areas or which have comparatively little influence upon the growth of the village or its opportunities for serving the surrounding areas: church or chapel, clinic, library, primary school, post office, shop, public house, garage or agricultural engineer, allotments, public water supply, electricity, gas, occasional bus services, village organizations such as Women's Institutes and men's clubs—one point each.

In addition, one point was allocated to each village for every hundred of its population. Points were totalled for each village and a classification of centres drawn up:

1. Principal villages and rural centres   — 90 points and over
2. Large villages   — 60-89 points
3. Medium villages   — 30-59 points
4. Small villages   — 20-29 points
5. Hamlets   — less than 20 points

Rural centres were distinguished, by the range of facilities they possessed, from principal villages which were largely residential or industrial in character. Apart from the problems involved in scoring facilities, the role played by a centre cannot be assessed simply in terms of number of facilities or size of local population. Moreover, one might disagree with the qualifying statements for groups A and B, especially with the premises that secondary school and village hall are significant factors attracting people to live in a village, and that a sewerage system and playing field are significant features in respect of the sphere of influence of a settlement. Even though at this time there was little settlement theory

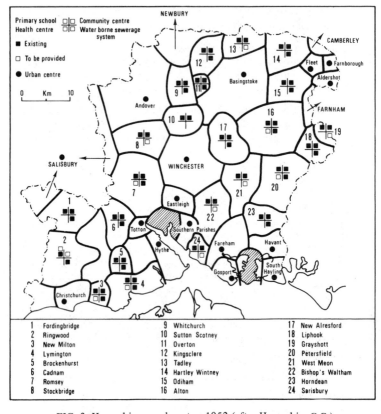

FIG. 3 Hampshire: rural centres 1952 (after Hampshire C.C.)

or few results of geographical research available for use by county planning authorities, it is difficult to explain such a confused interpretation of the functions and life in rural settlements.

The second illustration concerns the delimitation of the servicing area of settlements intended as centres for social, educational or health facilities. As part of the development plan, each county was obliged to identify such centres and to show their location on a county basis. Many settlements already had such functions and thus the location was predetermined; in areas without some of these functions an existing centre was often selected to supply them. There was, however, little assessment made of the quality of the services or of the population to be served and few counties showed the catchment area for each service. By contrast Hampshire (1955) identified centres and their catchment areas after consideration of factors like accessibility and distribution throughout the county (Fig. 3).

References

Bracey, H. E. (1953 and 1956) op. cit. p. 7 above.

Dickinson, R. E. (1947) op. cit. p. 7 above.

Dorset C.C. (1952). *County Development Plan–Report of the Survey.*

Hampshire C.C. (1955). *Development Plan–Written Statement.*

Hertfordshire C.C. (1951). *Survey Report and Analysis of County Development Plan.*

Lindsey C.C. (1952). *County Development Plan–Report of the Survey.*

Ministry of Town and Country Planning (1948a). *Circular 40–Survey Requirements for Development Plans,* H.M.S.O.

– (1948b). *Circular 59–Town and Country Planning (Development Plans) Regulations,* H.M.S.O.

–1950. *Notes on the Siting of Houses in Country Districts,* H.M.S.O.

Monmouthshire C.C. (1954). *County Development Plan–Report of Survey and Analysis.*

Scott Committee (1942). *Report of the Committee on Land Utilization in Rural Areas,* Cmnd. 6378, H.M.S.O.

Worcestershire C.C. (1951). *County Development Plan.*

Worcestershire C.C. (1973). *Worcestershire Structure Plan.*

4 Key settlements

Settlements selected as service centres ranged widely in size and in suitability for other functions. Hampshire made the important distinction that these centres were not necessarily suitable for residential development, the basic reason being that the factors influencing the location of service centres differed from those influencing the location of land for housing purposes. Thus evolved the concept of the *key settlement*, a concept which has been extensively used in many parts of Britain as a means of providing rural dwellers with essential services and facilities at reasonably accessible locations. Though widely applied, from areas of persistent depopulation to areas of continual growth, little research has been done on the success or failure of such settlements, and few planning departments have monitored their key settlement policies.

Key settlements are found in various forms. Some are essentially service centres, some are associated largely with public investment in facilities such as education or health and in council housing schemes, and others are associated with all types of residential development. In some counties key settlements are identified as possible growth points for industry and other forms of employment, but more generally industrial development is encouraged in larger rural settlements or market towns. In essence the principle behind the key settlement concept is one of concentration of limited financial resources upon a few selected centres rather than dispersal throughout a range of settlements. The concept has close affinities with threshold theory—the idea that a certain level of facility, like a health centre, is not economic below a certain threshold of population and that by grouping together a number of villages and hamlets, this critical threshold can be reached. The key settlement concept was proposed for the Cambridge Region in the inter-war period and was subsequently implemented in the form of the village college system. This scheme has had a considerable measure of success, partly due to the Cambridge region being a growth area and partly to the strict control of residential expansion in Cambridge itself. Key settlement policies are currently being applied in counties where depopulation is prevalent or where rationalization of the settlement pattern is deemed necessary. Devon and Berwickshire are two counties with such problems.

Devon put forward the idea of a key settlement policy in the first review of the development plan in 1964. It had been found that hitherto resources had not been used to advantage and that a fresh policy was needed. Such a policy had to take account of rural depopulation, the changing function of the village in relation to urban centres, the decline in agricultural employment and the need for alternative employment in towns, and the contraction of public transport. The key settlements selected were part of a more extensive settlement policy involving sub-regional centres, sub-urban towns, key inland towns and coastal resorts. The criteria used to select key settlements are worth quoting in full, particularly since Devon C.C. felt that the aims of the above policy could be achieved if major residential developments and new public utilities were permitted only in the key settlements. The selection of these settlements depended on:

1. Existing social facilities, including primary (and in some cases secondary) schools, shops, village hall and doctor's surgery, and public utilities (gas, water, electricity, sewerage).
2. Existing sources of employment (excluding agriculture) in or near the vicinity of a village.
3. Their location in relation to principal traffic roads and the possibility that new development may create a need for a by-pass.
4. Their location in relation to bus routes or railways providing adequate services.
5. Their location in relation to urban centres providing employment, secondary schools, medical facilities, shops and specialized facilities or services. (Key settlements are not appropriate near main urban centres.)
6. Their location in relation to other villages which will rely on them for some services.
7. The availability of public utilities capable of extension for new development.
8. The availability and agricultural value of land capable of development.
9. The effect on visual amenities.

Some sixty-eight key settlements were initially selected though these were reduced to sixty-five in the second review of the development plan in 1970. This report claims considerable success for the policy based on the fact that the rate of rural depopulation in north and mid-Devon fell from 254 per year in 1951-61 to 63 per year in the first four years of the operation of the policy. However, the report also makes the point that of the new housing completed between 1964 and 1968, 17·4 per cent was in the key settlements, compared to 22·5 per cent in other villages. Quite clearly, some of this 22·5 per cent was given permission before the policy was applied, and by the period 1966-71 this proportion had fallen to about 13 per cent, as against 17 per cent in key settlements.

On the facilities side, it is equally difficult to measure the effectiveness of the policy: in primary education the proportion of pupils being educated in key settlements rose from 39·8 per cent in 1961 to 44·0 per cent in 1971; but in 1972 forty-eight of the key settlements were listed as needing immediate improvements to sewage disposal works, a factor which should hinder residential development. However, the operation of such a policy in a large county like Devon is naturally a long-term process, not one that can be wholly effective in a decade and even if rural depopulation continues in some parts, many village groups have benefitted from the improved facilities and amenities that have so far been constructed in the key settlements. If the trends in population change continue in the 1970s it is likely that all rural districts in Devon will show increases in population, which will greatly aid the economic provision of modern services and facilities.

Berwickshire stands in marked contrast to Devon in that all its landward, i.e. rural, districts are declining in population and very few centres are increasing significantly. In 1972 the County Council was proposing to implement a policy concentrating public investment for infrastructure and housing in a number of so-called growth points. Such growth points are in effect key settlements, providing services and employment for people from the surrounding areas, and essentially only growing in respect of new housing for migrant people from the rural parts of the county. The dilemma for Berwickshire lies in the need to stem its absolute population decline and to provide, against this falling population base, modern facilities for those remaining. The policy proposed is to delimit groups of villages and hamlets, each group having a key centre where some expansion might be realized. Four of these centres are outside the county boundaries, a point which recognizes the importance of functional relationships rather than administrative divisions. The groupings are illustrated in Fig. 4.

The working of the proposed policy can be summarized with reference to the Duns settlement group. The main priority is to attract industry into the town of Duns, whose role will be to provide the work opportunities and housing for the group. The County Council consider that all new investment by the local authority should be injected into Duns and not to the other settlements in the meantime. Swinton, a planned village, has conservation as its main policy with redevelopment of the derelict sites preferably undertaken by private developers. For the other five settlements 'there should be no deliberate investment in new projects . . . by the local authority', although private development would not be precluded. In such a situation, which is common in many parts of the Border country, the key settlement policy is perhaps the only realistic

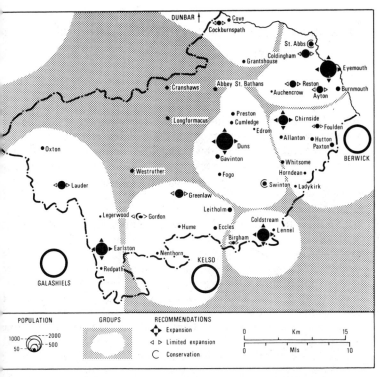

FIG. 4 Berwickshire: settlement groups 1972 (after Berwickshire C.C.)

alternative. If the key centres are to succeed, it will be at the expense of the other settlements in the group since population catchments are low and thresholds for services and facilities relatively high.

The reader will have appreciated that key settlements are not solely service centres but are also associated with the location of residential development. This additional function is in accordance with the principle that residential development is best located, in economic terms, in settlements with a range of essential services and facilities. This review now turns to a consideration of policies relating to residential development and to a discussion of the different settlement classifications which have evolved over the post-war period.

References

Berwickshire C.C. (1972). *A Rural Policy for Berwickshire.* Draft Report.
Devon C.C. (1964). *Development Plan (First Review)—Analysis of the Survey.*
— (1970). *The County Development Plan (The County Area) (Second Review)— Analysis of the Survey.*

5 Residential development and settlemen classifications

In the first development plans most attention in respect of housing and potential residential land was centred on the urban areas. Even in the essentially rural counties the towns and market centres were covered in some depth and had town maps prepared, whereas housing in the villag and hamlets often had scant mention. Some counties, Lancashire for example, were so overwhelmed by the urgency of urban problems that rural policies were not formulated until the first review of the develop- ment plan. Other counties, where growth of population created pressui for development land, dealt with rural settlements very superficially, treating many of them simply as sources of land for residential purpose Twenty-five years later, some of these counties still do not have any sy tematic form of rural settlement policy, other than statements relating to conservation areas, despite instructions to the contrary from central government.

There were some exceptions: Cambridgeshire (1952) submitted tow maps for groups of villages around Cambridge, in which were indicated both scale of growth and acreage of land required. This approach of complementary growth in surrounding villages in order to restrain expa sion of the city was unusual in its use of the functional relationship between town and country. It also showed an appreciation that in the following decades the dormitory function of villages was likely to be- come stronger and expand to include villages increasingly distant from the city. Such clear, integrated plans for residential development laid tl foundation for more comprehensive policies involving a new village, de tailed village plans and the character and design of new development in villages. The problems are by no means solved since the rural districts around Cambridge are areas of accelerating population growth, and cor sultants have recently reported with proposals for a fresh approach bas on a 'cluster dispersal' strategy for growth (Parry Lewis 1974).

Monmouthshire also recognized the possible implications of dormit growth and was probably the first county to classify settlements in respe residential development. The classification was a simple three-category o

1. Villages and/or hamlets which are shown diagrammatically on th County Map as being major centres in which development will be encouraged.

2. Villages and/or hamlets, not shown on the County Map, in which development will also be encouraged.
3. Villages and/or hamlets in which applications for further development will be considered on their individual merits.

Such an unconditional policy may well have been appropriate for the early 1950s in rural Monmouthshire; it is questionable whether this policy is sufficiently adaptable for the complex patterns of growth to be found in districts of accelerated population increase, which is the current trend in Monmouthshire.

Outside the growth areas, the majority of development plans followed the advice given in the various circulars: policies aimed at concentrating new residential development in towns or the major centres, at providing council housing in the villages where it was needed, and generally restricting sporadic building in the open countryside other than where it was required for agricultural or forestry workers. A number of county councils were more adventurous in their policies, often for very good reasons: Durham recognized the importance of restructuring its settlement pattern in accordance with modern needs and with changing employment locations. This controversial policy of restructuring has been discussed in depth elsewhere (Blowers 1972) and it is sufficient here to include, for comparison with other classifications outlined later in this chapter, the settlement categories on which the policy was based. Four types of settlement were recognized, each with its own policy:

1. Those in which the investment of considerable further amounts of capital is envisaged because of an expected future regrouping of population, or because it is anticipated that the future natural increase in population will be retained.
2. Those in which it is believed that the population will remain at approximately the present level for many years to come. It is felt that sufficient capital should be invested in these communities to cater for approximately the present population.
3. Those from which it is believed there may be an outward movement of some part of the population. In these cases it is felt that only sufficient capital should be invested to cater for the needs of a reduced population.
4. Those from which a considerable loss of population may be expected. In these cases it is felt that there should be no further investment of capital on any considerable scale, and that any proposal to invest capital should be carefully examined. This generally means that when the existing houses become uninhabitable they should be replaced elsewhere, and that any expenditure on facilities and services in these communities which would involve public

money should be limited to conform to what appears to be the possible future life of existing property in the community.

Needless to say, the controversy arose over the category 4 villages although the development plan analysis clearly stated: 'There is no proposal to demolish any village, nor is there a policy against genuine village life. It is proposed to remould gradually the pattern of development in the interests of the County as a whole.'

Almost all county councils put forward policies restricting development outside nucleated settlements although the 1950 advice note did not advocate rigid policies for scattered development, but rather implied that applications for isolated houses should be considered on their merit. A later Policy Note (M.H.L.G. 1969), however, stated that in open country new houses would not be allowed unless there were special circumstances, and that even isolated groups of housing would not normally be permitted additional development. The trend has been for policies to apply positively to nucleated settlements only, disregarding any dispersed groupings. Such an approach has been adopted in many parishes, where proportionately the number of dwellings in dispersed forms exceed those in the nucleated settlement. A method of analyzing and classifying such non-nucleated settlement together with models of possible future forms could be valuable for both policies and plans.

A further feature of the immediate post-war period was the control on housing development through a licensing system. Most houses were built by local authorities and very few by private developers, and it was during this period of control that the statutory development plans were prepared and formulated. Many of the policies put forward at this time were heavily reliant on Ministry advice and envisaged a period of continued economic restraint, tight controls on land for development and little population migration or mobility. Furthermore, the problems of rural areas took second place to those in the towns and cities.

During the late 1950s and the 1960s many planning authorities found that increasing attention had to be paid towards residential development in villages where private builders were enlarging their share of house construction. With primary employment contracting, the social structure of the village was changing rapidly and this, linked with the growth in personal mobility and the consequent widening of the housing market, made it necessary to rethink the role and function of the village. Increasingly the village became part of the urban region, reliant on the town for shopping, entertainment, and employment, and as a possible source of building land for residential purposes. In the early to mid-1960s the quinquennial reviews of the statutory development plans were undertaken and more integrated settlement policies began to evolve. It is evident from these reviews that positive measures to control and guide residential development were seen as essential and that many villages could not just be left to develop but had to be planned in some detail.

The policies put forward in the course of the reviews, often published later in separate reports, tended to be in the form of settlement classifications. But a new methodology was also advanced, namely, an assessment of the village based on factors for and factors against residential development. To the geographer, this approach offered a new method of analyzing rural settlements and, at the same time, suggested probable directions in which the settlement pattern for a county or subregion might evolve in the future. Not all the factors considered were spatial ones but their implications almost always had a spatial expression.

The background research to such classifications consisted of a village by village survey, sometimes based on field survey, sometimes based merely on local authority records, but more often than not on both, together with a subjective evaluation of the strength of the constraints on, or potential for, development. In some cases, the factors appeared as part of the classification, e.g. Huntingdonshire (1962):

Class 1   Villages in which expansion is unlikely within the development plan period
           Reasons: low probability of growth because of remoteness—
                       lack of services—education deficiencies—primarily
                       agricultural
Class 2   Villages where expansion is limited to either agricultural necessity or minor infilling
           Reasons: on a principal traffic route—in the Green Belt—
                       lack of services—education deficiencies—other
                       special factors (flooding and drainage)—special
                       architectural or landscape character—
                       conservation of agricultural land
Class 3   Villages where expansion is deferred
           Reasons: by-pass proposed—sewerage and surface water
                       drainage proposed—water supply proposed
Class 4   Villages suitable for minor expansion
           Reasons: services available—special architectural or land-
                       scape character—physical limitations
Class 5   Villages suitable for major expansion
           Reasons: accommodation needs (centralization of local
                       authority housing)—services available—wide
                       physical limitations—high probability of growth
                       because of proximity to large centres

Although each village was summarized in respect of the balance of factors, no indication of expected population increases was given and there was no quantitative expression of minor or major expansion, but simply a

statement that major and minor are used in relation to the existing size
of the village.

In 1967 the Ministry of Housing and Local Government (M.H.L.G.
1967) issued a planning bulletin on settlement in the countryside. Its
aim was to assist the formulation of policy and the preparation of settlement plans, and it released settlement policies and plans from the confines of the statutory development plan system. Local authorities were
advised that settlement policies should include:

1. An approximate estimate of the future population planned for . . .
   broken down to show the implications of policies of restriction or
   expansion applying to groups of villages.
2. Lists of settlements to be expanded substantially or tightly restricted, with a statement of the criteria on which the decisions are based
3. Special policies, e.g. for the establishment of new settlements, or
   for restraint in villages of exceptional quality.
4. In accordance with Circular 50/57, for Green Belt areas, a list of
   villages where limited infilling is proposed.
5. Development control policies applying generally in villages and the
   countryside.

With this advice and a theoretical example, settlement classifications were
prepared in a more coherent manner than hitherto. West Suffolk (1968)
produced a factor-by-factor analysis in map form and summarized these
in diagrammatic form for each of its six rural districts (Table 10). The
ultimate policy class for any settlement could be one of five, but it is not
clear how factors were weighed against each other, as a perusal of the
table and the classification will indicate. The five classes were:

Category A: Villages where growth would be inappropriate because
               of the situation and structure of the existing settlement
               and where planning applications will be adjudged solely
               on local needs. There will be cases where the Planning
               Committees will determine that no further growth is
               desirable in the general interest of the settlement.

Category B: Villages where a limited amount of land may be released
               for development, but where the decision will be influ-
               enced by local needs and no further land will be zoned
               in the village plan.

Category C: Villages where limited areas of land may be released for
               housing in a phased programme of development, taking
               into account the varying factors relating to each village.

Category D: Villages where development will be encouraged to take
               place in accordance with a phased programme. These
               villages will be regarded as key villages in the rural
               settlement pattern.

Source: West Suffolk C.C. 1968

Factors influencing residential development – Melford R.D., West Suffolk

Villages and policy class:

No.	Village	Policy class
1	ACTON	D
2	ALPHETON	A
3	ASSINGTON	B
4	BOXTED	A
5	BURES ST. MARY	C
6	CHILTON	A
7	GLEMSFORD	D
8	GREAT WALDINGFIELD	D
9	HARTEST	B
10	LAWSHALL	B
11	LEAVENHEATH	D
12	LITTLE CORNARD	A
13	LITTLE WALDINGFIELD	B
14	LONG MELFORD	E
15	NAYLAND	B
16	NEWTON	A
17	SHIMPLING	B
18	SOMERTON	A
19	STANSTEAD	A
20	STOKE-BY-NAYLAND	B

× indicates factors relevant

Factors against

Factor	1	2	3	4	5	6	7	8	9	10	11	12	13	14	15	16	17	18	19	20
ESTATE VILLAGE OR 2/3 OWNERS			×																×	
PARISH WITH OUTSTANDING VILLAGE										×				×	×				×	
SETTLEMENT IN A.O.N.B.															×				×	
20% DWELLINGS LISTED										×				×	×				×	
DISPERSED SETTLEMENT												×	×	×						
LINEAR SETTLEMENT ON PRIMARY ROAD				×			×							×						
ACCIDENT AREA OR OVERLOADED PRIMARY ROAD																				
NO SECONDARY SERVICES				×	×													×		
4 OR LESS PRIMARY SERVICES		×	×	×	×					×	×	×						×	×	
SCHOOL: POSSIBLE CLOSURE OR REMODEL NEEDED						×			×					×			×			
SCHOOLS OVERLOADED															×					
MUCH MORE LAND FOR GROWTH THAN BEFORE									×	×										
POPULATION LOSS 1951–67	×		×						×									×	×	×
POPULATION 200 OR LESS			×															×		

Factors for

Factor	1	2	3	4	5	6	7	8	9	10	11	12	13	14	15	16	17	18	19	20
POPULATION 1,000+							×							×	×					
POPULATION 50% GAIN 1951–67																				
LESS LAND AVAILABLE TO MATCH PAST GROWTH				×									×		×		×		×	×
SCHOOLS: SPARE CAPACITY				×					×								×			
SCHOOL: NEW / IMPROVED EXISTING OR PLANNED								×						×						
8–10 PRIMARY SERVICES							×							×	×					×
3–4 SECONDARY SERVICES			×		×									×	×					×
MAIN RADIAL TO URBAN CENTRE			×											×	×					
BY-PASS PLANNED CLUSTER SETTLEMENT	×		×	×		×				×							×			×
9% OR LESS DWELLINGS LISTED	×		×	×	×	×			×	×	×	×						×		
30 MINUTES TO IPSWICH/COLCHESTER		×		×											×	×				×
SCHOOL: EXISTING SECONDARY OR PLANNED MIDDLE																			×	×

Category E: These small country towns require special consideratio
and the policies have already been largely determined
and approved plans prepared.

In addition to this classification, which was similar to policies adopted
in Norfolk and East Suffolk, the analysis took note of the advice in the
planning bulletin with respect to villages of exceptional quality and ident
ified those which were of outstanding character either nationally or locally

Not all counties were as thorough as West Suffolk, especially those
which had a number of urban areas to deal with: the West Riding of
Yorkshire carried out planning studies on a rural district basis, in the
course of which account was taken of the influence of the larger towns
and cities and of the impact of policies outside the rural district, like the
Leeds-Bradford Green Belt. There was not a factor-by-factor approach,
the resultant classification being drawn up on the significance of village
character and scale of residential development (West Riding 1967).

Reports and studies on sub-areas below the county level increased in
number in the late 1960s: Nottinghamshire, Northamptonshire, Durham
and the North Riding of Yorkshire all published policy reports for either
functional areas or rural districts. In contrast to those for the West Ridin
some of these studies defined the future distribution of population with
respect to selected villages and included outline village plans and village
development areas. The approach in Durham (no date) was to assess, for
selected villages, those sites where planning permission had been given
but which had not been developed (committed development) and those
sites which could be developed without detriment to the village's character (potential development). Future population increases could then be
calculated. With such details, a tiered settlement policy was not really
necessary and these studies superceded the earlier policy classifications.
But the problem that remained was whether the available sites in the
selected villages were sufficient in total to meet the estimated demands
for housing in the sub-area or rural district. In both the districts studied,
the sites identified were more than adequate in relation to expected
increases. Clearly an approach like this needs periodic reviews or, better
still, continual monitoring because there is no assurance that land will
come onto the market in line with the planning authority's expectations
The hope is that developers, or potential sellers of land, would be guided
or perhaps encouraged by the identification of sites in these plans.

Northamptonshire (1965–72) in a similar set of plans for urban sub-
areas and rural districts, distributed the anticipated population among
three classes of village—key centres, villages for moderate expansion, and
villages for limited growth. In the light of what has already been said
about the interpretation of these qualitative terms, it is interesting to
note that there is a fair degree of consistency in the scale of growth

expected among these three types. For example, in Towcester R.D. over the period 1967-81, scale of growth and ultimate populations were to be as follows:

1. The key centre was expected to show over 100 per cent increase to a population of 6000.
2. Villages for moderate expansion were to show over 50 per cent growth to populations between 600 and 3000.
3. Villages for limited growth were to have less than 50 per cent growth, in the majority of cases less than 30 per cent, with ultimate populations of 100 to 550.

Not every planning authority would agree with Northamptonshire in this interpretation of moderate expansion and limited growth, but it is the prerogative of every authority to choose its own scales and rates of change. However, the method of approach to residential development is important, not so much for the sub-region's or district's future pattern of population, as for any particular village. Durham and Northamptonshire considered the individual village, but there are cases where the sub-regional growth is considered first and sites searched for at village level afterwards. The planning policy for the Salisbury sub-region fits into this type of approach. In 1968 Wiltshire undertook a study of the sub-region and concluded that a growth of some 18 000 population was likely in the period up to 1981 (Wiltshire 1970). This expected population is to be accommodated in accordance with the settlement classification for the area:

A Small towns and large villages which, by virtue of their local communications, services and education facilities—available or proposed—are suitable for expansion without adversely affecting the character of the area or the settlement itself.

The four settlements in this group were together expected to take some 10 000 population, though the proportion expected in any one settlement was not stated.

B Villages provide some facilities to a surrounding community and are suitable for limited development without adversely affecting the character of the settlement or the area.

These settlements—ten in number—should take 2700 population, though again individual proportions were not stated.

C Villages and hamlets which by reason of their character and/or lack of facilities will be limited to infilling of small sites within the existing settlement framework.

These forty-two villages or hamlets were to take 1800 population.

The remaining 3500 population was to be accommodated within Salisbury itself (Fig. 5). The rural settlements were planned to accept some 80 per cent of the sub-regional growth but none of the villages have site plans

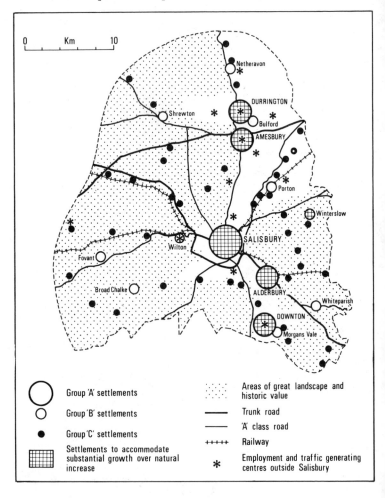

FIG. 5 Wiltshire: Salisbury sub-region–proposals 1970 (after Wiltshire C.C.)

as yet and the classification above was based on services and facilities
rather than potential for residential development. Another defect of this
'superimposed approach' is that the classification ignores past patterns of
of change in the villages and this, combined with the lack of information
on proportions of future growth, makes it extremely difficult for any
village to know what lies in store for it. Some of the villages in the A and
B categories have increased by over 50 per cent in the past decade and
would perhaps welcome a period of little change to enable their

populations to stabilize socially. At a time when public participation in planning is being encouraged and when public interest in the living environment and amenity in general is growing, the social and demographic structure of the village needs to be considered as well as the functional characteristics.

By contrast, some planning authorities have formally recognized that villages, and small towns for that matter, have capacities, which may be conditioned by physical limitations (such as steep slopes), or by size of utilities and facilities (such as sewerage and education). These capacities allow villages to go through cycles of change and in some policy classifications these cycles have been incorporated and phasing or timing of change recognized. Huntingdon and Peterborough updated the 1962 classification in this way, and the policy for the Isle of Wight (1968) is similar. For example, in Huntingdon and Peterborough (1972), category B (minor growth) settlements include villages 'where development will be on a modest scale . . . as consolidation of previous expansion schemes', and in category C (limited development) there are villages 'where expansion is considered to be complete, or deferred beyond the next 10–15 years'. Though a more exact comprehension of a village's structure may have to wait until a detailed study or appraisal can be made, these attempts show that some authorities are prepared to look more closely at individual settlements rather than simply at the sub-regional or county distribution patterns.

Whilst considerable attention has been paid in regional and urban planning to theoretical strategies and locations of growth, in rural planning there has been very little. Apart from proposals like the Hampshire rural centres and key settlements in Devon, there is little evidence to show that authorities have considered spatial relationships for residential development. If we look at a typical distribution pattern of different classes of growth around an urban centre—that around Shrewsbury shown in Fig. 6—there seems to be little symmetry or recognizable arrangement of the A and B class locations. The planning authority makes no mention of an orderly location for the different classes of settlement; there is no attempt to think out a theoretical arrangement and fit this to the pattern of settlements in the sub-region. There are several reasons why an ordered arrangement is desirable: to allow residential development to be spread evenly throughout the sub-region, to avoid competition between locations of the same class, to allow an ordered pattern of services to develop, and to prevent problems arising elsewhere. Taking the Shrewsbury example and dividing the villages within a ten-mile radius according to quadrant, the following distribution is found.

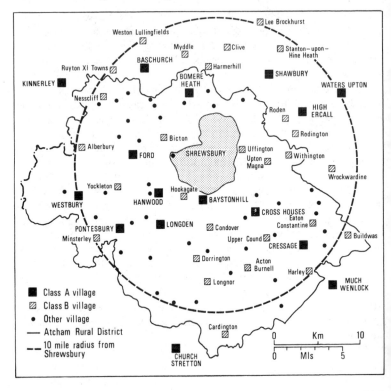

FIG. 6 Shropshire: Shrewsbury district--village policy 1970 (after Salop C.C.)

	A class villages	B class villages
North-West	3	7
North-East	3	7
South-East	2	6
South-West	5	6

It can be seen that whilst the B class locations (minor expansion) are evenly spread, the A class locations (major expansion) are unevenly placed especially in the South-West. Here there are three locations for substantial expansion within three miles of each other. Furthermore, the average distance from Shrewsbury for both classes of village is just over six miles, whereas it might be expected that the A class settlements would be, on average, further out than the B class ones. Moreover, at rural district level

TABLE 11

Population trends and ratio of policy classes in Shropshire

Rural district	Pop. trend	% change 1961–71	Size of pop. change	Ratio of A to B class villages
Clun and Bishops Castle	Reduced depopulation	−9·3	−905	1 : 2·5
North Shropshire	Reversed depopulation	1·7	516	1 : 4·5
Oswestry	Reversed depopulation	1·9	579	1 : 1·8
Ludlow	Reversed depopulation	2·8	642	1 : 2·6
Market Drayton	Reversed depopulation	8·6	1332	1 : 4
Atcham	Reversed depopulation	16·6	3741	1 : 2
Bridgnorth	Accelerated growth	8·5	2496	1 : 2·6
Shifnal	Accelerated growth	19·5	2590	1 : 5
Wellington	Accelerated growth	25·2	6112	1 : 2·7

Source: Salop C.C. and census 1971

there is little consistency between population trends and the ratio of A and B class settlements (Table 11). Villages have been classified according to their suitability for expansion and not in relation to changes in population distribution (Salop 1971). This brief analysis of the policy for one county in isolation is not intended to give the impression that the policy is incorrect or is unlikely to work but that there appear to be some spatial inconsistencies and that a theoretical approach might be worthy of some consideration. Quite clearly there is scope for geographical research in this field.

In comparison, it is worth looking at the methodology used in the preparation of policies for rural settlements in Warwickshire (1973) as a part of the county structure plan. The steps in the procedure were:

1. To determine how much growth is appropriate in the rural areas.
2. To examine every settlement over 200 population to see where the growth can best be located.
3. To consider the existing commitments, and
4. to draw these three stages together to determine which settlements should take the bulk of the future growth.

It had already been decided that future developments should be concentrated in certain key settlements which were to absorb not only their own natural increase of population but also some from the villages in their hinterlands. At the same time such settlements were to be developed to act as service centres for these hinterlands. The aim of the exercise was to identify the key settlements, and this was done under three

headings—development potential, land constraints and commitments.
For each of 154 settlements fourteen factors were analyzed and measured
such as landscape, residential visual environment, primary schools and
various means of accessibility, all of which had some bearing on the
development potential. These factors were scored in a range of 0–5 and
then four different weightings representing different objectives were
applied to the factors. Fig. 7 shows one of these strategies, that with a
particular emphasis on the economics of development with high weighting
on the conservation of good farmland and the availability of sewerage.
The settlements have been divided into four groups according to their
ranking under this strategy. Those settlements appearing in the higher
rankings in three or more strategies were considered as possible key
settlements. Similar scoring, based on a consideration of eight criteria,
was carried out for land constraints. Finally, the amounts of land already
allocated for development were summarized in rank order of size. Since
such land was already committed for development, the settlements with
the largest areas were used as a basis for the selection of key settlements.
Thus it could be said that the key settlements were pre-determined, but
the development potential analysis was used to confirm that these were
suitable for growth. The ten settlements with the largest commitments
became the first-tier key settlements having a policy of moderate expansion of over 1000 persons by 1986 (Fig. 8). These ten did not meet the
scale of growth expected in all districts in the county and so another—
Polesworth—was added. Because the geographical distribution was also
somewhat uneven, eight second-tier key settlements were selected to
take modest expansions of between 100 and 500 persons. Some of the
settlements considered for this second tier had moderate commitments
but were not designated as such because of low development potentials.
Others, without significant commitments, were upgraded on the grounds
of high development potential scores or few land constraints and these
filled in the remaining distributional gaps. And, finally, some were
excluded because they were located close to key settlements already
selected, for example, Mancetter and Baxterley. Comparison of Figs. 7
and 8 will indicate that considerable sifting and rationalizing has been
necessary to arrive at the final distribution. In general, this distribution
is related to estimated population increases and, whilst there may be
certain deficiencies in the details of the analyses, the policies seem to
have a much sounder spatial base than is the case in other counties.

  Discussion so far on residential development policies has largely
concerned the rural areas undergoing some pressure and has ignored
remoter rural areas. In general, counties with large stretches of remote
countryside and isolated settlements can be grouped into three classes:

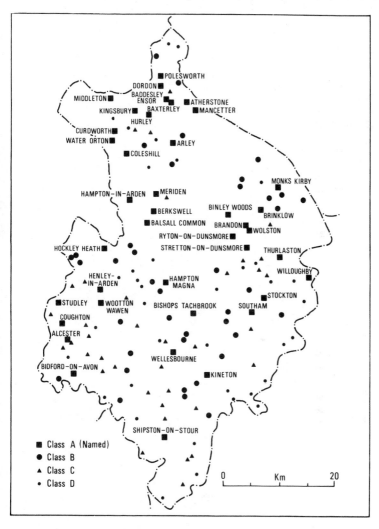

FIG. 7 Warwickshire: strategy 1–development potential classes 1973 (after
        Warwickshire C.C.)

1. Those with a very rudimentary policy or with no policy at all in an
   areal sense.
2. Those with a simple two- or three-class policy aimed at rationalizing the settlement pattern.
3. Those with a more sophisticated policy occasionally linked with
   the theory of growth points or employment centres.

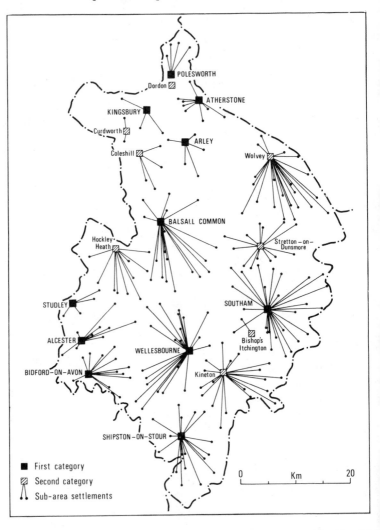

FIG. 8 Warwickshire: key settlements and sub-areas 1973 (after Warwickshire C.C.)

Little further need be mentioned about the first group except to add that the nature of the settlement pattern in these areas, together with the configuration of administrative boundaries, has led to policies and plans for individual settlements rather than for an area as a whole. In the second group the policies tend to be limited to development associated with agriculture, forestry or occasionally tourism. Residential development is not very likely because there is out-migration of young people and there is little in-migration or commuting to larger centres. Denbighshire (1969) has recognized these facts and operates a two-class policy:

1. Villages selected as rural centres where the provision of village facilities will be encouraged and residential development consolidated.
2. Settlements where limited residential development only may be appropriate.

The aim of this policy is to bring about improvements in facilities and services and to ensure that the character of the areas is maintained and enhanced, given the limited economic opportunities that exist.

The third group includes counties such as Northumberland, Roxburgh and Caithness. Northumberland (1969) has based its policy on the small towns acting as 'anchorage points' of employment and new housing; below these are smaller centres in the interstitial rural zones outside the catchment areas of the towns, which are seen as 'supporting growth points'; and at the lower level are 'consolidation points' for the concentration of housing to serve the needs of the smaller scattered communities.

In the Caithness Development Plan Review (1974) six strategies were put forward, based on different scales of economic growth and varying conservation controls linked with tourist development. The alternatives ranged from strict control of development in the landward areas with major growth at the centres of Wick and Thurso, to small-scale growth up to existing capacities in Wick and Thurso with a graded system of control in the rural areas. This study illustrates very clearly the restricted choice open to such remote regions even with the possibility of oil-related developments.

The Southern Uplands of Scotland have had severe problems of accelerating depopulation though in some parts, like Roxburghshire, the small towns and some villages are now experiencing moderate increases. Having accepted the recommendations in the Central Borders Plan—an addition of 25 000 people by 1980 throughout the region—Roxburghshire (no date) formulated a policy for population and housing in the rural areas to take account of this future growth and also of past trends. The basic approach was to classify settlements in terms of their inherent growth potential, assessed through factors such as location, demographic structure and local authority housing demands, and to relate this classification to other factors such as physical restrictions, land quality, amenity and service capacities. Furthermore, settlements were examined in groups associated with each of the four burghs of Kelso, Melrose, Jedburgh, and Hawick. The ultimate policy categories are seen as guidelines for areas 'which in present circumstances would appear to be most suitable for public investment and those areas in which future developments would seem to be on such a small scale that major outlay would not be justified.' The categories are as follows:

A Settlements which are suitable for considerable expansion. In these settlements development will probably substantially alter the existing character of the settlement. This will mean that considerable expenditure will need to be committed, and that cost threshold will be of less significance than in settlements where more limited growth is proposed.

B Settlements which are suitable for moderate expansion, but where the basic existing village form will not be affected. These villages should be developed to their existing thresholds, and beyond if the scale of development would justify this.

    1. Settlements where this scale of growth would be desirable, and on the basis of existing and future trends can reasonably be expected to be achieved.

    2. Settlements where this scale of growth would be desirable, but where on the basis of existing trends and future prospects so far as they can be estimated, it cannot at present be considered likely.

C Settlements where expansion should be mainly in the form of minor infilling, rounding-off and essential redevelopment, and where considerable capital expenditure in relation to the expansion of the village involving the crossing of the thresholds should be avoided. (This does not mean that expenditure considered necessary for the improvement of facilities for the existing population should be avoided.)

This group may again be divided into two:

    1. Villages which could be allowed to grow by rounding-off, infilling and other limited forms of development within their existing thresholds.

    2. Villages which should be strictly controlled as to their future growth or where even the limited development mentioned above seems unlikely in present circumstances.

This type of policy classification is rather similar to that proposed for Durham in 1951 but the geographical circumstances are very different.

Though directed towards the location of public investment in infrastructure and housing, the policy report covers many other aspects including private development, housing tenure and the possibilities of development in the small scattered communities in the county. If population trends continue to follow the pattern of the last two decades, this is the type of policy which will have to be thought out in many other remote rural regions where as yet policies are particularly sketchy or non-existent.

Over the period since 1947 policies expressed in the form of settlement classifications have been of major significance for rural settlements. Whatever form the settlement pattern eventually takes, the effect of these graded, or hierarchical, policies will be very evident in many counties. There is, in addition, a further set of policies, which have already had marked impacts in some areas, and which deserve a brief mention and it is to these that this study now turns.

References

Blowers, A. (1972). 'The declining villages of County Durham', in *Social Geography*, Open University, 143–57.

Caithness C.C. (1974). *Review of the County Development Plan–Interim Report.*

Cambridgeshire C.C. (1952). *Development Plan–Report and Written Analyais (Part One).*

Denbighshire C.C. (1969). *Planning Area 3, Clwyd–Appraisal and Planning Policy.*

Durham C.C. (no date). *Village Studies: Stockton R.D., Barnard Castle R.D.*

Huntingdonshire C.C. (1962). *A Rural Policy for Huntingdonshire.*

Huntingdon and Peterborough C.C. (1972). *Rural Settlement Planning Policy.*

Isle of Wight C.C. (1968). *A Rural Policy for the Isle of Wight (Part One).*

Ministry of Housing and Local Government (1967). *Settlement in the Countryside–a planning method*, Planning Bulletin 8, H.M.S.O.

– (1969). *Development in Rural Areas*, Development Control Policy Note 4, H.M.S.O.

Northamptonshire C.C. (1965–72). *A Plan for Rural Development.* In 7 parts (e.g. Part 7: Plan for Towcester R.D.).

Northumberland C.C. (1969). *Rural Northumberland–Report 2, Policy for Growth and Concentration.*

Office of Population Censuses and Surveys, *Census 1971.*

Parry Lewis, J. (1974). *A study of the Cambridge Sub-region,* H.M.S.O.

Roxburghshire C.C. (no date). *Landward Community Development Strategy.*

Salop C.C. (1971). *Housing Development in Rural Shropshire.*

Warwickshire C.C. (1973). *County Structure Plan–Supplementary Report 5, Rural Settlements.*

West Riding of Yorkshire C.C. (1967). *Wetherby Rural District Map Report.*

West Suffolk C.C. (1968). *West Suffolk Rural Planning (Part Two).*

Wiltshire C.C. (1970). *Salisbury Sub-regional Study.*

6 Zoning and conservation policies

Many county councils have operated zoning policies, some of which have had pronounced effects on the settlement pattern and on the development of particular villages. These zoning policies can be divided into two types: policies which have been designed specifically as constraints on development—such as Green Belts—and policies which have been concerned largely with landscape conservation, such as those relating to national parks and areas of great landscape value. Often these areas and the particular zoning policies overlap each other. This does not necessarily imply that controls are increased accordingly, since in essence the policies have similar effects on villages and hamlets differing mainly in respect of control on other forms of development. In general, these policies place limitations on the scale and location of new residential development.

When the Green Belt concept was introduced in the mid-1950s, its aim was to restrict the outward spread of urban areas, to prevent nearby towns merging and to preserve the special character of a town. Within the Green Belt itself, however, the aim was to maintain, and hopefully to enhance, the rural character not only of the open landscape but also of the many villages that were situated within it. But contrary to widespread opinion, development is and has been allowed within Green Belts under a system of 'excluded' or 'excepted' villages. Kent (1972) operates the system under which certain excluded settlements have been defined as being suitable for development within the confines of the existing built-up area, but villages which have not been excluded are subject to the overall Green Belt policy. This means that development will be restricted to:

1. That directly related to agriculture.
2. The provision of educational or recreational facilities.
3. Certain types of open development such as hospitals and other institutions with large grounds.

In Surrey, the policy is similar but greater emphasis is placed on the appearance of the settlements: 'it is intended to control development so as to preserve the charm and character . . . and to this end, to permit only such development as may be required in connection with the needs of the rural community and limited infilling which, in both style and layout, will be worthy of its setting.' (Surrey 1971). Surrey, also, have realized that many problems related to settlement planning arise within the area of the Green Belt itself and have had to draw up policies in respect of size of dwellings, enlargement of country cottages, replacement of existing dwellings and new agricultural dwellings.

It is evident that the original aims of Green Belts have brought about unplanned social changes within the Green Belt itself as a consequence of the preservation of country zones immediately adjacent to an urban area. A Green Belt has become a desirable area in which to live and from which major, or even minor, changes have been excluded. There is, however, very little in county policy statements about the provision of council houses or housing of modest value to retain the social character of Green Belt villages, and it is undoubtedly true that some villages have become almost entirely one-class (i.e. professional class) settlements. On the other hand, it is these social groups who are motivated towards and who possess the financial resources for maintaining the traditional outward charm and character.

A number of planning authorities have operated 'Green Belt type' policies around some of their growing urban centres. An interesting example is from Northamptonshire (1965), where two sorts of Green Belt were proposed around the town of Northampton. The inner 'dark green' zone, about two miles wide, had strict controls on residential development in the eleven villages it contained, while in the outer 'light green' zone restrictions were less stringent and allowed more flexibility of growth through natural increase. At the outer boundary of the 'light green' zone were located the key settlements which were planned to take major increases in population. Thus the operation of the green zones was complementary to the growth of the key settlements.

Around the city of Aberdeen two types of restricted area have been proposed—one a formal Green Belt, the other an outer area with a 'safe-guarding policy' designed to give greater control over the pressures for isolated sporadic residential development outside the nucleated settlements (Aberdeen 1973). Both these examples indicate that there seems to be a need for two types of constraint zone, one to prevent urban extension, the other to maintain the character of the open countryside and restrain development which may leapfrog the inner belt.

The second group of policies concerning landscape conservation have not been as marked in their effects as have Green Belt policies. In general, the designation of areas of great landscape beauty and of high amenity value has been one factor deterring major expansion from the settlements lying within them, though limited development and minor growth have been regarded as acceptable. This is well illustrated by the proposals for growth in the Salisbury sub-region (Fig. 5), where the major (A class) development locations lie adjacent to but not within the areas of great landscape value. The extent to which such growth locations are controlled by landscape quality is difficult to assess since many planning authorities tend to lay more stress on the value of the townscapes of the settlements than on the setting (Wiltshire 1970).

Nevertheless, it is a fact that many areas of great landscape value contain, on average, a greater proportion of attractive villages than non-designated landscapes. This is evident in Kesteven (1969) where the County Conservation Policy lists some fifteen out of eighteen villages as having special character along Lincoln Cliff, an area of great landscape value, but in the Trent Vale to the west only eight out of thirty are listed. The salient aspects for policy purposes tend to be the design and enhancement of village character, though the Peak Park Planning Board (1975) has endeavoured to control the quantity of new development and relate it to local needs rather than to commuter demand from the Sheffield area. As with Green Belts, preservation policies for high quality landscape areas may bring about housing demands, which in their turn tend to find various outlets for which additional controls may be necessary. Thus some policies create a need for further policies.

Further restrictive policies have been applied to countryside zones where recreation or tourism have been regarded as of some importance. In such areas, policies have emphasized the significance of leisure activities as well as the necessity of strictly controlling any changes within the fabric of the settlements. The point often made is that such settlements are part of the attraction of the area, that their inherent character is a part of the tourist sector of the area's economy, and therefore new development should be carefully controlled. Examples of areas where such policies apply include the fishing villages of Cornwall, villages in National Parks, and the string of villages along the Avon Valley in Worcestershire where 'it has become apparent that it is necessary to restrict growth in many villages in order to conserve and enhance their character. More restrictive alternative policies are being suggested for consideration in the County Structure Plan.' (Worcestershire 1972). The policy classification covering the Avon Valley villages is given below; worthy of note is that whilst development is not excluded, its scale and design are given particular emphasis; the number of villages in each category is in parenthesis:

1. Villages for special protection. Villages in this category are not for development and should have special protection because of their small size, their appearance, and situation. House building in such villages would only be permitted in special circumstances and even then great care would be necessary in the design and layout of new buildings. (2)

2. Other villages not proposed for development. Villages in this category do not quality for special protection because of their situation, or

appearance, but are still considered unsuitable for anything more than limited infilling in scale with the existing development. (9)

3. Villages for limited development but needing special protection. This category applies to larger villages of special character where development will require special care in siting and design to harmonize with the existing village. (5)

4. Other villages for limited development. This category is for the villages where some estate development would not be considered inappropriate but which do not have the special character of villages in category 3. (3)

The main criticisms of such classifications revolve around the subjective assessment of village character and the rigidity of the policies, especially those relating to villages in category 2.

In Chapters 3—6 the aim has been to illustrate the range of policies which have been devised for the planning of rural settlement at either the county or district level. It is clear that many aspects of these policies have a distinct spatial expression and are of interest to the rural geographer. Though little theory has been utilized in the preparation of these policies, it is evident from recently published structure plan reports that planning authorities are improving their approaches to and methodology for understanding rural settlement structures and systems.

References

Aberdeen C.C. (1973). *Aberdeen Area—Interim Policy Statement.*
Kent C.C. (1972). *Development Plan (1967 Revision): Amendment to Written Statement.*
Kesteven C.C. (1969). *County Conservation Policy.*
Northamptonshire C.C. (1965). *A Plan for Rural Development—Part 1a.*
Peak Park Joint Planning Board (1975). *Annual Report 1974—75.*
Surrey C.C. (1971). *Development Plan Written Statement.*
Wiltshire C.C. (1970). *Salisbury Sub-regional Study.*
Worcestershire C.C. (1972). *The Avon Valley*

7 Policies and plans at village level

Many of the settlement policies prepared at county level have formed an integral part of statutory development plans. By contrast, most of the plans and policies for individual rural settlements have not had ministerial approval but are approved county council policy. As with county level policies, little theory is available to aid village plan preparation though governmental advice (M.H.L.G. 1967) outlined the principles to be followed. Since the policies and proposals contained in published village plans are wide-ranging, this chapter will concentrate on the approaches used in these plans. The practical problems of planning villages have been discussed comprehensively by Thorburn (1971).

Very few village plans were produced as part of the county development plans but by the first review several counties had prepared outline plans, especially for villages likely to be affected by residential growth. Not all counties have prepared village plans, for a variety of reasons: some have argued that plans are not necessary for every village, some prefer to judge development applications on their merits rather than against a pre-conceived plan, and others suggest that village plans encourage development. It seems to be generally agreed that plans should be drawn up only where necessary, such as for villages with a policy of expansion, villages with infrastructural or renewal problems, villages requiring conservation measures, or for new villages. For other settlements or areas of dispersed housing, short policy statements are seen as sufficient for the purposes of development control.

Five basic approaches have been employed in village plans: the outline structure (or layout-design) approach, the capacity (or envelope) approach, the visual appraisal approach, and the policy area and conservation area approaches. Many plans are combinations of two or more approaches, such as those for Cambridgeshire villages (1970–71).

The outline structure approach

The form and layout of rural settlements have long been of interest to the historical geographer, and it is surprising that more attention has not been given by the planner to this feature of the village. The tendency has been to allow development which would help to infill, to round off or to form the neat, compact village. The result has been that the original structure has not been obliterated so much as enclosed, whereas it might have been augmented and enhanced. Capacity and envelope approaches have been responsible for this enclosure process, though some planning authorities are now attaching more importance to outline structure in determining conservation areas within and around villages. However, not all planning authorities were slow to see the importance of the physical structure: in 1952 Durham issued a report on building in the countryside in which there were examples of different types of village based on their layout and structure, together with suggestions as to how the villages could have been better developed. Sharp (1953) examined the structure of the village as a contributory factor in forming a social unit, and showed by example what could be achieved by an understanding of the form of the ground plan. And, perhaps, the most significant example of the outline structure approach was in his plans for the new Forestry Commission villages in Northumberland, where he proposed layouts which had a strong traditional form about them (Sharp 1955).

Many county councils found that, for a number of reasons, an outline structure approach would not work in villages under the normal process of development control. For this approach to have any degree of success it had to be applied as part of a comprehensive plan for the village with development programmed to completion, otherwise there could be no assurance that the structure would ultimately be achieved in the form desired. Another reason was that the land required did not necessarily come on the market in the appropriate sites and blocks to allow a pre-conceived structure to evolve; furthermore, private developers had their own ideas about new form and layouts in villages; and finally, it could be argued that the social needs which produced the traditional form do not apply today and that the mid-twentieth century should leave its own peculiar imprint on the village.

This approach has been used, though not widely, and its application has been, in general, to parts of a village rather than the whole. Essex (1970) has recently pioneered anew the problems of design and layout through 'design briefs' for new housing areas in villages, and Warwickshire (1971b) has also prepared planning briefs for selected parts of some of its larger villages; both stress the point that new structures should acknowledge the traditional and at the same time take advantage of any existing characteristics on the site itself. The idea of using open space or community buildings as focal points for the overall structure is one method by which the traditional village structure can be extended. This has been the approach in the Civic Trust reports (1969) on Cheshire villages.

New development, it is stated, may be divided into four categories, all of which have some bearing on the outline structure:

the extension of the old village core by consolidation with new per-
imeter development,
the infill site, i.e. the consolidation of the existing close-knit character,
the establishment of a definite edge to the village, and
the forming or retention of a village green together with the encouragement of social amenities.

In each of the three case studies, for villages of different policy groups,
new village greens are suggested, as well as short rows of terraced housing,
to produce a feeling of enclosure and continuity, which are not achieved
through block or estate developments.

Capacity approaches

The defining of village capacities and limits has formed a major part
of development control policies in village plans, and this type of approach
has been widely used. The reasons for capacities or limits are varied, but
they often relate to problems such as the outward spread of residential
development and the overloading of services and utilities. No clear meth-
odological approach is apparent in the way in which village limits and
spatial capacities have been defined, and there are some notable differences in the methods employed, particularly in the perception of the
village edge. For example, some authorities have maintained that a village
should end abruptly, and that if natural boundaries to a village do not
exist, they should be created. Others have argued that a village should
gradually merge into the landscape and that away from the village centre
the density and scale of development should decrease. The imposition of
firm boundaries may be unrealistic when the natural limits are a combi-
nation of open, diffuse or distinct edges. On the other hand, there may
be very sound reasons for limits to override natural features as, for
example, when it is desirable to restrict residential development to one
side of a main traffic route.

The capacity approach most frequently used has been that of the
village envelope, known by a variety of terms—village development limit,
planning limit, development boundary, village area or village curtilage.
The most common use of the envelope has been to delineate the outer
edge of a village beyond which residential development is not allowed.
Some envelopes have included potential residential sites, thus allowing
further growth of the village; others are more restrictive, being drawn
around existing properties allowing only infilling of single plots within
the village structure. Such applications of the envelope approach conform to the objectives of rounding off, infilling and consolidation, and
to the evolution of compact villages with little regard paid to the overall
structure of the village or to the density or spatial character within the

structure. Other useful objectives for an envelope approach have been to prevent nearby settlements from merging with one another and to encourage infilling of land between separated parts of a village. Since the delineation implies change within, and little or no change without, some plans have deliberately excluded part of the village from the envelope in order to safeguard and improve the character of it, which seems to be a curious way for conservation to be carried out.

A criticism of the envelope method as an expression of a village's capacity is that it implies that all the land within is suitable for development. This might have been true on some of the early envelope plans, but planning authorities have had to add qualifications to the policy to correct this impression. Planning Bulletin 8 (M.H.L.G. 1967) suggested that there might be permanent and temporary development boundaries around a village. This point has been used in some village plans, notably in Worcestershire (1972). The areas with provisional boundaries may be extended when most of the designated sites are completed within the village; this is therefore a more flexible approach than the ultimate development limit.

Another criticism of the envelope approach is that it should be related to the thresholds of utilities or capabilities of services and facilities in the village. Such thresholds or capacities are not easily determined but certain ones have been used, like sewerage system and primary school, to calculate the upper population capacity of the village (Aberdeen 1972). In some plans, development is programmed in a series of phases, thus allowing the settlement to grow, in theory, slowly and steadily, the phasing being related to the provision of services and facilities.

Both forms of capacity delineation seem to be going out of favour with planning authorities, who are now moving in the direction of visual appraisals and problem-orientated plans. The capacity approaches have served their purpose in many villages to retain compactness, to enable authorities to assess land availability in a sub-region or county, and to ease the burden of development control. But they have brought about changes which have altered the character and destroyed the essential structure of many villages for which more recent plans are having to apologize.

Visual appraisal approach

Under this heading can be included other types of appraisal such as physical appraisal and landscape appraisal, but generally all emphasize the theme of the visible components of the village. Visual appraisals are not plans, though the features distinguished by this method can influence proposals made in a plan and also, by helping to define objectives, can shape the policies required. Some of the most thorough visual appraisals have been carried out in connection with policies for conservation areas, particularly those for historic towns and areas of outstanding architectural quality. Rural planning authorities were slow to include visual assessments in their village plans though many had recognized the architectural and amenity value of villages and towns in the first development plans. Somerset (1964) listed towns and villages of amenity value in the development plan survey (Fig. 9) and also noted villages with churches of special interest. But it was not until the late 1960s and 1970s that detailed surveys were being carried out to analyze the character of a village and assess it such that effective measures could be taken to conserve or enhance it.

Kent (1969), together with Essex and Cambridgeshire, developed the visual appraisal method very successfully, in as much as the intrinsic quality of the village can be readily appreciated. The village studies in Kent have managed to do this through a systematic area-by-area description with sketches; maps locate the visual assets, the visual detractions and the possible improvements. Under visual assets are such features as important buildings, grassed areas and important trees, views, visual barriers and important focal groups, while the visual detractions include untidy areas, buildings needing attention, stretches of wirescape and poles, and locations of objectionable signs and advertisements. Improvement of these features is implied as other improvements are itemized separately, such as new fences, walls or hedges. In addition each study contains lists of the buildings of architectural and historic interest together with a short description of each. This form of appraisal is concerned with the appearance and charm of each village and, although only carried out for selected villages, portrays a more sympathetic attitude towards the village than is found in many village plans. Other planning authorities have built on the experience of counties like Kent and have developed their own particular methods. Some have felt that certain villages deserve a building-by-building treatment, especially if it is part of a designated conservation area. An example of this is Warwickshire's (1970) townscape study of Shipston-on-Stour. Each street in the central area is analyzed through the facets of its character, and problems and areas for improvement are identified. The detail is brought together in a series of townscape maps showing an assessment of overall qualities in three grades, important features and suggestions for enhancement. Some of this visual appraisal is finally written into the planning guidelines for the town centre.

Not every village or small centre demands this degree of attention though many plans are now tending to include some form of evaluation of character. Whilst most visual appraisals have been made by planning

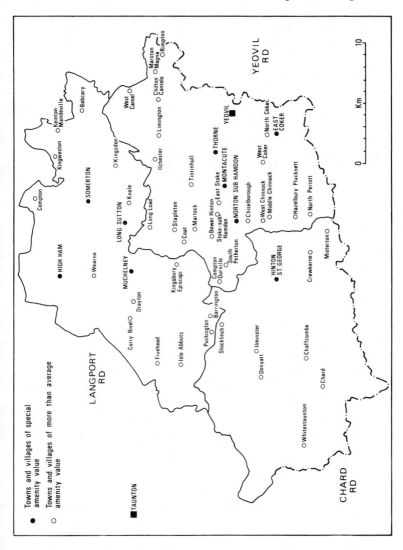

FIG. 9
Somerset: towns
and villages of
high amenity
value 1964
(after Somerset
C.C.)

departments or consultants, it is a field in which local civic and amenity groups can participate. Already some groups have carried out projects, such as the Weald of Kent Preservation Society (1970).

Policy areas and character areas

Rural settlements, as a rule, tend not to have clear morphological units unless they are relatively large or have expanded markedly in recent years. Nevertheless, several planning departments have sub-divided villages into character areas or identity areas, though mainly for the purposes of survey and description rather than for policy-making. The major exception to this is the 'conservation area', an area distinguished by its architectural quality and to which stricter planning policies apply. There are, however, some differences between counties in their approach to the process of sub-division. Most of the plans, which have used the character area approach have distinguished initially the core or focus of the village and then delineated the other sectors of the village on the basis of periods of growth or structural form. Depending on the purpose of the division, the whole of the village may be covered, or just parts of it. If the objective is conservation, it is likely that only the older areas will be included, but if it is design policies, the whole village together with potential residential sites might be assessed. Some authorities, recognizing that in small villages the term 'character area' is inappropriate, have used 'component area' (Dorset 1973); such areas are not architecturally distinct so much as spatially separated.

Conservation areas lend themselves to more qualitative sub-divisions: in Blandford Forum (Dorset 1970a), three basic identity areas with subsections were differentiated in the town centre:

1. Areas of national importance, e.g. grand eighteenth-century urban.
2. Areas of prime importance, e.g. nineteenth-century town houses.
3. Areas of secondary importance, e.g. rural domestic housing.

A somewhat different approach is the identification of 'action areas', as in Totnes (Devon 1972), where some fourteen areas were the subject of detailed recommendations in respect of improvements.

Planning Bulletin 8 put forward the idea that, where necessary, special policy areas, like action areas, should be defined in village plans. Few planning authorities have done this formally but the plans for Cambridgeshire villages have comprehensively used the policy area approach. For separate parts of the villages an appropriate policy is outlined, including areas not yet developed for which particular design and layout policies are specified (Fig. 10).

This approach is more useful in the larger villages than the smaller ones, or in villages where changes are having spatially differentiated

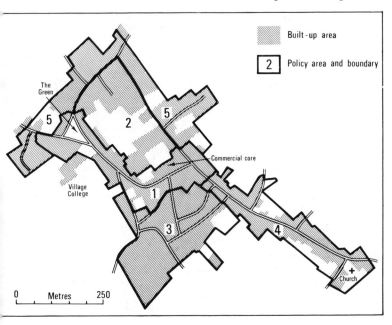

FIG. 10 Cambridgeshire: Cottenham village plan—policy areas 1970 (after
        Cambridge C.C.)

effects. A further use of both identity area and policy area approaches
may be found in plans for new villages, such as New Ash Green, where
the structure is composed of separate neighbourhoods.

Conservation Areas

Conservation Areas are special policy areas resulting from the Civic
Amenities Act of 1967. Prior to this date conservation policies mainly
concerned buildings of special architectural and historic interest (listed
buildings); since the emphasis was on individual buildings, policies tended
to overlook the surroundings or setting of the buildings and the overall
character of the village. Accordingly, the 1967 Act was directed towards
areas rather than buildings. It required local planning authorities to
determined areas of special architectural or historic interest, the character of which it is desirable to preserve or enhance, and designate such
areas as 'Conservation Areas'. Since 1967 over four thousand areas have
been designated in urban and rural settlements.

The aims of Conservation Area policies are similar in principle
throughout the country:

1. the safeguarding of listed buildings and other buildings contributing to the character of the area, both by statutory powers and by the use of grants and loans for improvements to or repair and maintenance of important buildings;
2. a closer control over new development by insisting on detailed designs or sketches before any decision is given; particular attention will be given to materials and colours, building lines and height;
3. a more critical assessment of existing development, including advertisements and 'permitted development';
4. a greater attention to details—street furniture, signs, poles, wires and lighting can all detract from the appearance of an area; statutory undertakers, local authorities and developers will be encouraged to give priority to minimizing clutter and unsightliness;
5. local effort and initiative from individuals or local societies must be encouraged. (East Suffolk 1971).

The Ministry circular (53/67) relating to the Act stated that the designation of an area was only the first stage and that this should consist of a survey to decide the boundary of the area, reasons for designation and an analysis of building groups and features which make special contributions to the area. The second stage would be the formulation of policies for the detailed control of development and of positive plans for enhancement of the character of the area. This preparatory stage has varied from a rapid appraisal of such features as listed buildings, trees and the main area of architectural quality (East Sussex 1969) to detailed townscape studies identifying aspects that require further study and attention (East Sussex 1972). Where action for preservation or improvement has been urgent, survey and analysis has been selective, as in the study of Boddam, a decaying fishing village on the coast near Peterhead (Aberdeen 1971). Here the Conservation Area has been divided into grade I and grade II parts. The grade I zone has been studied in depth, items for treatment have been selected, costs have been estimated and money set aside for improvement works. The grade II area, where the problems are not so great, will be studied in the near future. Because conservation is costly, priorities for improvements and enhancement will have to be established, and this may well be a difficult third stage in the conservation process.

The areas designated may vary considerably. Most rural Conservation Areas cover the older core of a village, but some have been drawn so as to include the whole of a village (Dorset 1970b). Occasionally an area of open land is included, especially if it is an historic feature or if the open land is an integral feature of the settlement (East Lothian 1974). Some authorities have recognized a fringe area around the Conservation Area to ensure that adjacent developments are not detrimental to the designated area (Somerset 1970).

Conservation as a process does not end at the boundaries of the designated areas, and several planning authorities have issued policy statements on conservation in the wider context. Some of these relate to the design, materials and colours preferred in new developments over a wide area (Peak Park Planning Board 1964); others are specific to a village locality (Warwickshire 1971a). Such guidance and consultation are vital for conservation policies to work effectively but the success of Conservation Areas will be measured by the visible improvements and enhancements that are made.

Some conclusions

It is evident that in the past decade many village plans have been prepared to accommodate residential development in accordance with some form of settlement classification. But more recently some authorities have initiated problem-orientated plans and designed policies to operate at village levels. It seems that this trend will continue, particularly with the greater emphasis now being placed on conservation measures and with the growing interest in the environment. The type of plan now being prepared by planning authorities, such as Cambridgeshire, shows not only a comprehensive approach but also a clear understanding of the problems of the village. The most obvious gap in nearly all village plans is information on social and demographic aspects such as migration, age-structure, use of services and social facilities. Type and quality of housing is another area in which little work has been done; this topic is closely allied to social characteristics and the two could well be investigated together.

Finally, it is interesting to note that a number of enterprising parish councils are now preparing their own plans, policies or appraisals. The basic problem here is whether such studies will be acceptable to the local planning authority in order that the plans can be adopted as a part of district policy. But, with a little co-operation and guidance, there seems to be no valid reason why village people should not be involved in planning their local environment (Salisbury District Council 1975).

References

Aberdeen C.C. (1971). *Boddam Conservation Area Report.*
– (1972). *Blackburn Village Study* and *Plan.*
Cambridgeshire and Isle of Ely C.C. *Cottenham Village Plan* (1970), *Bottisham Draft Village Plan* (1971), and *Linton Village Plan* (1971).
Civic Trust for the North West (1969). *Cheshire Villages–an environmental vocabulary.*
Devon C.C. (1972). *Totnes Conservation Study.*
Dorset C.C. (1970a). *Blandford Forum- Conserve and Enhance,* report by D. W. Insall and Associates.
  (1970b). *Milton Abbas Conservation Area.*

Dorset C.C. (1973). *Sydling St. Nicholas–Development and Conservation.*

Durham C.C. (1952). *Buildings in the Countryside.*

East Lothian C.C. (1974). *County Planning Policy.* Reference to Gifford Conservation Area.

East Suffolk C.C. (1971). *Needham Market–Policy Statement and Planning Proposals.*

East Sussex C.C. (1969). *Alfriston–Designation Report.*

– (1972). *Hurstpierpoint Conservation Report.*

Essex C.C. (1970). *Newport Village Study–Consultation Plan.*

Kent C.C. (1969). *Village Study–Biddenden.*

Ministry of Housing and Local Government (1967). *Settlement in the Countryside,* Planning Bulletin 8, H.M.S.O.

Peak Park Planning Board (1964). *Building in the Peak.*

Salisbury District Council (1975) with Pitton and Farley Parish Council: *Pitton– a planning study.*

Sharp, T. (1953). 'The English Village', in *Design in Town and Village,* H.M.S.O.

– (1955). 'Forest villages in Northumberland', *Town Planning Review,* 26, 165–70.

Somerset C.C. (1964). *Development Plan (First Review)–Written Statement.*

– (1970). *Axbridge Conservation Area.*

Thorburn, A. (1971). *'Planning Villages',* Estates Gazette.

Warwickshire C.C. (1970). *Shipston-on-Stour–a Local Plan.*

– (1971a). *Bidford-on-Avon–Design and Materials for the Locality.*

– (1971b). *Shipston-on-Stour–Planning Brief for Area D.*

Weald of Kent Preservation Society (1970). *Stone-in-Oxney–a Village Study.*

Worcestershire C.C. (1972). *Offenham Village Plan.*

8 Future trends

It is clear that since 1947 the aims and types of rural settlement policies and plans—relating to expansion, rationalization and conservation—have not changed in principle although the emphasis given to any particular one has altered. Where the emphasis will, or should, in future lie is not easy to predict. There is evidence that in a number of city regions the outward movement of population to rural areas is steadying and may well stabilize, whereas in the intermediate rural areas the peak of population growth may be yet to come. In more remote areas, apart from a few persistent pockets of depopulation, it appears that population contraction is easing and totals are stabilizing, and may even increase. But wherever the emphasis is placed, it seems likely that, for a number of reasons, the rural parts of Britain will feature more in the planning process in future than they have in the past. There have been recent alterations in the framework for planning: firstly in the form of the development plan system, and secondly in local government organization. The new development plans (structure plans and local plans) should allow consideration of rural settlements within a broader context in respect of planning aims, policies and proposals; in addition, individual settlement plans, which in principle should express in detail the structure plan strategies, will take the form of integrated local plans. The new district units of local government administration, since they are larger than the former rural districts, have recognized broader functional areas. Whether these framework changes will create more effective development control in relation to policies will emerge in due course.

In the last five years a number of planning authorities have been slowly adjusting their policies and plans to fit in with the new frameworks. Hampshire, for example, has recently published district plans, like those for Lymington and Winchester, which have been prepared and designed as local plans. A new feature in these plans is the consideration of alternative forms and directions that future development might take, together with an evaluation. Another adjustment that planning authorities will make in future is the consideration of particular problems or policy themes. To some extent, this has already been operating in the field of recreation and conservation, but has not yet penetrated settlement planning. However, Denbighshire has set a trend with planning reports on second homes and rural housing, but there are other topics which will require consideration, such as council housing in villages, the appearance of and control over farm buildings, redundant churches and other disused buildings, and the impact of tourism and weekend recreation on villages. There is little doubt that the emphasis on conservation will continue with more detailed and positive studies on those settlements of significant historic and architectural value, such as the recent report by Hampshire on the market centre of Romsey. Finally, there may well be more attention paid to the possibility of new villages; though currently not in favour as a means of accommodating population growth in rural areas, new villages may eventually be recognized as a creative and feasible alternative to the continual expansion of existing settlements. They may also be seen as socially desirable.

As a conclusion it would seem useful to attempt to identify where geographically-based research could make a contribution to the planning of rural settlements. It has been stressed that much of the post-war planning of rural settlement has been done without a sound, well-researched theoretical base and in this respect there are three themes worthy of investigation.

1. The spatial distribution of population growth around urban centres, considering different scales of growth and its phasing over varying periods of time, with a view to constructing alternative models of development location.
2. The changing morphological character and structure of villages in different policy classes in order to produce models and theories of village development under planned conditions.
3. The identification, measurement and analysis of the spatial character of settlements intermediate between strongly-nucleated and clearly-dispersed types.

Further work, but non-theoretical, could include monitoring of new development both at the sub-area level and within the framework of any village or parish. Following on from this topic there is the possibility of investigating the effectiveness of policies in relation to their aims; this would not be a specifically geographical task but clearly would include spatial elements and have some spatial expression.

References

Denbighshire C.C. *Second Homes in Denbighshire* (1972), and *Rural Housing* (1974).

Hampshire C.C. *Winchester and District Study* (1974), *Lymington District Plan* (1972), and *Romsey Conservation Study* (no date).

Ministry of Housing and Local Government (1970). *Development Plans—A Manual on Form and Content.*

Index